W9-BCT-400

Team Spirit

Clifton Park - Halfmoon Public Library
475 Moe Road
Clifton Park, New York 12065

THE TEXAS RANGERS

BY

MARK STEWART

Content Consultant
James L. Gates, Jr.
Library Director
National Baseball Hall of Fame and Museum

NORWOOD HOUSE PRESS

CHICAGO, ILLINOIS

Norwood House Press
P.O. Box 316598
Chicago, Illinois 60631

For information regarding Norwood House Press, please visit our website at:
www.norwoodhousepress.com or call 866-565-2900.

All photos courtesy of Getty Images except the following:
Topps, Inc. (6, 14, 20, 34 top & bottom right, 35 top left, 37, 41 top, 43);
Black Book archives (21, 22 bottom, 23 top, 36, 39,); TCMA Ltd. (34 bottom left);
SSPC (40 top & bottom left); Author's collection (40 bottom).
Cover photo by Lisa Blumenfeld/Getty Images.
Special thanks to Topps, Inc.

Editor: Mike Kennedy
Designer: Ron Jaffe
Project Management: Black Book Partners, LLC.
Special thanks to Jerry Crausbay, Merri Lynne Alexander, and Tom Bosworth.

Library of Congress Cataloging-in-Publication Data

Stewart, Mark, 1960-
    The Texas Rangers / by Mark Stewart ; content consultant, James L.
Gates, Jr.
        p. cm. -- (Team spirit)
    Summary: "Presents the history, accomplishments and key personalities of
the Texas Rangers baseball team. Includes timelines, quotes, maps, glossary
and website"--Provided by publisher.
    Includes bibliographical references and index.
    ISBN-13: 978-1-59953-176-2 (library edition : alk. paper)
    ISBN-10: 1-59953-176-3 (library edition : alk. paper) 1. Texas Rangers
(Baseball team)--History--Juvenile literature. I. Gates, James L. II.
Title.
GV875.T4S84 2008
796.357'6409764531--dc22
                                                        2007043508

© 2008 by Norwood House Press.
Team Spirit™
All rights reserved.
No part of this book may be reproduced without written permission from the publisher.
••
The Texas Rangers is a registered trademark of Southwest Sports Group, Inc.
Major League Baseball trademarks and copyrights are used
with permission of Major League Baseball Properties, Inc.

Manufactured in the United States of America.

3727

COVER PHOTO: The Rangers celebrate a home run during the 2007 season.

Table of Contents

SPORTS WORDS & VOCABULARY WORDS: In this book, you will find many words that are new to you. You may also see familiar words used in new ways. The glossary on page 46 gives the meanings of baseball words, as well as "everyday" words that have special baseball meanings. These words appear in **bold type** throughout the book. The glossary on page 47 gives the meanings of vocabulary words that are not related to baseball. They appear in ***bold italic type*** throughout the book.

Meet the Rangers

Game-winning home runs, amazing catches, great **comebacks**, **no-hitters**—those are the calling cards of the Texas Rangers, one of the most exciting teams in baseball. No victory is out of reach when the Rangers play, and no lead is safe when their hitters are at home plate.

The Rangers draw crowds from the cities of Dallas and Fort Worth, as well as from other parts of Texas. The team's fans have become very attached to their favorite players—and *vice versa*. Many of the Rangers' stars have come back to Texas after playing for other teams. A few have come back twice!

This book tells the story of the Rangers. They began life in the nation's capital and then moved to the Lone Star State. They have had legendary stars and have been part of history-making games. Through all of their ups and downs, the Rangers have always played exciting baseball.

The Rangers congratulate each other after a win in 2007.

Way Back When

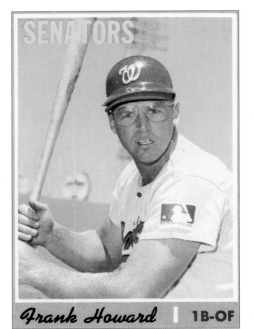

Frank Howard | 1B-OF

T he Rangers are one of two teams that were once called the Washington Senators. (The other is the Minnesota Twins.) In 1961, the Senators moved to Minnesota after 60 seasons in Washington, D.C. A brand-new team—also called the Senators— replaced them in the nation's capital. Baseball fans who rooted for the Senators in 1960 rooted for an entirely different group of Senators in 1961!

The new Senators were made up of unwanted players from other clubs. The team found a few diamonds in the rough, including pitchers Claude Osteen and Ron Kline, and hitters Chuck Hinton and Don Lock. A trade with the Los Angeles Dodgers in 1964 brought Frank Howard to the Senators. He became one of the most feared **sluggers** in baseball.

The team's first winning season came in 1969. The Senators hired former **All-Star** Ted Williams to be their manager. Williams

LEFT: A trading card of slugger Frank Howard.
RIGHT: Fergie Jenkins looks in for a sign. He won 25 games in 1974.

was a great student—and teacher—of hitting. The team's batting average soared, and Washington improved from 65 wins to 86. Unfortunately, the Senators did not keep improving. Soon they were looking for a new home.

In 1972, the team moved from Washington to Arlington, Texas and became the Rangers. Since the club did not have a lot of great hitters, it focused on pitching. During the next *decade*, the Rangers had some of the best pitchers in baseball, including Fergie Jenkins, Gaylord Perry, Jim Bibby, Bert Blyleven, Doc Medich, Jon Matlack, and Charlie Hough.

By the late 1970s, the Rangers were also a good team at the plate. Their offense was led by Buddy Bell, Al Oliver, Mike Hargrove,

Toby Harrah, and Richie Zisk. In the 1980s, more talented hitters joined the team. Larry Parrish, Pete O'Brien, Gary Ward, Ruben Sierra, and Pete Incaviglia gave Texas fans something to cheer about as the team tried to reach the **playoffs** for the first time.

Finally, in the 1990s, the Rangers became true *contenders*. The team's top two stars were Ivan Rodriguez, the league's best catcher, and Juan Gonzalez, a dangerous slugger who was named the **Most Valuable Player (MVP)** in the **American League (AL)** twice. Rodriguez and Gonzalez were surrounded by smart, hardworking teammates such as Will Clark, Rusty Greer, and Mark McLemore.

In 1996, 1998, and 1999, Texas finished with the best record in the **AL West**. Unfortunately, each time they fell short of the pennant. But Texas fans were still excited. The Rangers had taken the first step toward a championship by establishing a winning *tradition*.

LEFT: Ivan Rodriguez, the leader of the great Texas teams of the 1990s.
ABOVE: Juan Gonzalez, winner of the AL MVP in 1996 and 1998.

The Team Today

During the 1990s, the Rangers learned what it takes to play winning baseball. Championship teams have strong pitching and defense, **clutch hitting**, good leadership, and smart coaches and managers. Most of all, a winning team needs a core of young, homegrown talent.

The Rangers used that *strategy* to build a winning club for the 21st *century*. Young hitting stars Michael Young, Hank Blalock, and Mark Teixeira joined a group of **veterans** that included Alex Rodriguez and later Alfonso Soriano. Some of these players were kept as building blocks. Others were traded to fill other needs, such as pitching.

As the Rangers look ahead, they feel very confident about their chances to build a winner. The team is focused on putting together the right mix of pitching and hitting, young and old players, and stars and **role players**. Texas fans can look forward to a lot of good baseball in the years to come.

Hank Blalock and Michael Young celebrate during a 2007 game.

Home Turf

In their first year as the Senators, the team played in Griffith Stadium. For the rest of their time in Washington, the Senators played in D.C. Stadium. It was renamed Robert F. Kennedy Memorial Stadium in 1968.

The first home of the Rangers after moving to Texas was Arlington Stadium. It was built into the ground, so fans would enter from the top of the stadium and walk down to their seats. In 1994, the Rangers moved to the Ballpark at Arlington. It combines an old-time stadium feel with many modern features. The stadium is totally enclosed except for a narrow space in right field. It would take a perfect hit, but one day someone may launch a home run that completely leaves the stadium.

BY THE NUMBERS

- *There are 49,115 seats in the Rangers' stadium.*
- *The distance from home plate to the left field foul pole is 332 feet.*
- *The distance from home plate to the center field fence is 400 feet.*
- *The distance from home plate to the right field foul pole is 325 feet.*

A look at the Rangers' stadium from beyond the right field foul pole.

Dressed for Success

The 1960 Senators and 1961 Senators were completely different teams, yet they looked very similar on the field. Both teams wore white uniforms with blue pinstripes and red trim. The first big change to that style came in 1968, when red became the team's main color.

After the club moved to Texas and changed its name to the Rangers, the players went back to wearing red, white, and blue. The letter *T* replaced the letter *W* on their caps. The team's **logo** was the state of Texas with the initials *TR* on it.

TEXAS   3rd BASE

JIM
FREGOSI   RANGERS

The Rangers began using numbers on the front and back of their jerseys in the 1980s. By the 1990s, they had changed their uniform design to look more like it did in the 1960s—first the mostly blue style, and then the mostly red style. Today, the Rangers continue to wear uniforms that combine red, white, and blue.

Jim Fregosi models the Texas uniform from the 1970s.

UNIFORM BASICS

The baseball uniform has not changed much since the Rangers began playing. It has four main parts:

- a cap or batting helmet with a sun visor
- a top with a player's number on the back
- pants that reach down between the ankle and the knee
- stirrup-style socks

The uniform top sometimes has a player's name on the back. The team's name, city, or logo is usually on the front. Baseball teams wear light-colored uniforms when they play at home and darker styles when they play on the road.

For more than 100 years, baseball uniforms were made of wool *flannel* and were very baggy. This helped the sweat *evaporate* and gave players the freedom to move around. Today's uniforms are made of *synthetic* fabrics that stretch with players and keep them dry and cool.

Ian Kinsler takes the field in the Rangers' 2007 red, white, and blue home uniform.

We Won!

The Rangers were the best team in the AL West during the 1990s. They won four division championships from 1994 to 1999. The Rangers gave their fans plenty to cheer about, although they did not make it to their ultimate goal, the **World Series**.

The team's first division title came during the 1994 season, which was cut short by a dispute between the owners and players. Texas was in first place when the last game was played in August. The hitting stars of that team were Jose Canseco, Juan Gonzalez, Will Clark, and Ivan Rodriguez.

Two years later, the Rangers were back on top in

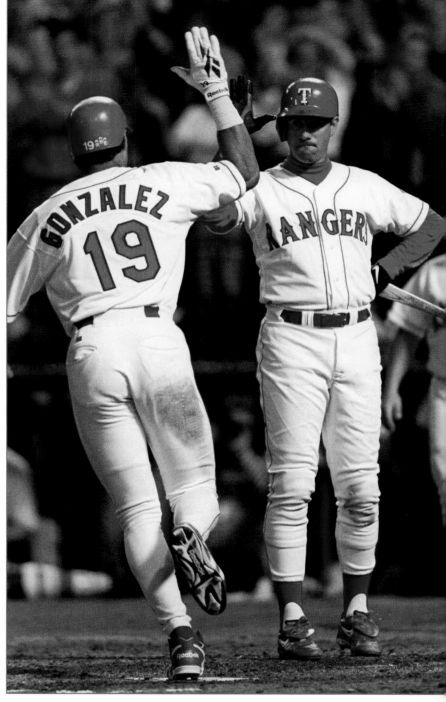

LEFT: Ivan Rodriguez gets his teammates fired up.
RIGHT: Will Clark congratulates Juan Gonzalez after a home run.

the AL West. Gonzalez, Rodriguez, and Clark led a powerful hitting attack that also included Dean Palmer, Rusty Greer, Kevin Elster, and Mickey Tettleton. In the playoffs against the New York Yankees, Gonzalez was unstoppable. He hit five home runs in four games. Rodriguez also played great baseball. After winning the opening game, however, the Rangers could not cool off the hot New York bats. The Yankees scored three comeback victories in a row to win the series.

The two teams played a rematch in the 1998 playoffs. Gonzalez, Rodriguez, and Clark led the hitting attack again, along with Greer and the Rangers' speedy new **leadoff batter**, Tom Goodwin. This time, each game was an exciting pitching duel. Despite its powerful **lineup**, Texas scored just one run in the entire series, and the Yankees won again.

The Rangers and Yankees met in the playoffs again in 1999. Rafael Palmeiro, who starred for Texas in the early 1990s, had rejoined the club. That season, he helped the Rangers bat .293 as a team, which was the highest average in baseball. Six different Rangers hit more than 20 homers. It looked like the year Texas would go all the way.

ABOVE: Rusty Greer reaches high over the fence to save a home run against the New York Yankees.

RIGHT: Rafael Palmeiro watches to see if his long drive clears the fence.

Rangers fans were hoping for a series with a lot of hitting. Instead, it was another battle of pitching, as the Texas bats were silenced once again. For the second year in a row, the Rangers scored just one run in a three-game defeat.

Even though the Rangers did not reach the World Series, the four AL West crowns collected by those teams in the 1990s gave them a special place in the history of Texas baseball.

The Rangers and their fans learned a valuable lesson. It takes great hitting *and* great pitching to win a championship.

Go-To Guys

To be a true star in baseball, you need more than a quick bat and a strong arm. You have to be a "go-to guy"—someone the manager wants on the pitcher's mound or in the batter's box when it matters most. Fans of the Senators and Rangers have had a lot to cheer about over the years, including these great stars …

THE PIONEERS

FRANK HOWARD   Outfielder/First Baseman

• BORN: 8/8/1936   • PLAYED FOR TEAM: 1965 TO 1972

Frank Howard was a huge man who looked like he could have played basketball. Not surprisingly, he hit the ball very hard and very far. Howard led the AL in home runs twice and **runs batted in (RBI)** once.

TOBY HARRAH   Shortstop/ Third Baseman

• BORN: 10/26/1948

• PLAYED FOR TEAM: 1969 TO 1978 & 1985 TO 1986

Toby Harrah was a very *patient* hitter. When he did see a pitch he liked, he often hit it a long way—especially for a shortstop.

ABOVE: Frank Howard
RIGHT: Nolan Ryan

JIM SUNDBERG — Catcher

- BORN: 5/18/1951   • PLAYED FOR TEAM: 1974 TO 1983 & 1988 TO 1989

Jim Sundberg was the best defensive catcher in the AL when he played for the Rangers. He won six **Gold Glove** awards in a row, beginning in 1976.

CHARLIE HOUGH — Pitcher

- BORN: 1/5/1948   • PLAYED FOR TEAM: 1980 TO 1990

Charlie Hough had a great **knuckleball**, and he used it to win 139 games for the Rangers. He was always among the AL leaders in games started, complete games, and innings pitched.

RUBEN SIERRA — Outfielder

- BORN: 10/6/1965   • PLAYED FOR TEAM: 1986 TO 1992, 2000 TO 2001 & 2003

Baseball came easily to Ruben Sierra. Within a few years of joining the Rangers at the age of 20, he led the AL in runs batted in. Sierra hit with power from both sides of the plate and had a cannon for an arm.

NOLAN RYAN — Pitcher

- BORN: 1/31/1947
- PLAYED FOR TEAM: 1989 TO 1993

Nolan Ryan was 42 years old when he joined the Rangers. Some wondered whether the hard-throwing pitcher could still get the job done. Ryan answered his critics by striking out 301 batters in his first season in Texas and pitching no-hitters in each of the next two seasons.

RAFAEL PALMEIRO — First Baseman/Designated Hitter

- BORN: 9/24/1964
- PLAYED FOR TEAM: 1989 TO 1993 & 1999 TO 2003

Rafael Palmeiro used his smooth swing to become one of baseball's finest hitters. He was also a very good first baseman. Palmeiro led the AL in hits in 1990 and doubles in 1991.

KENNY ROGERS — Pitcher

- BORN: 11/10/1964
- PLAYED FOR TEAM: 1989 TO 1995, 2000 TO 2002 & 2004 TO 2005

Kenny Rogers spent several seasons as a **relief pitcher** for Texas. When the Rangers made him a **starter** in 1993, he used his sinking fastball and **changeup** to win 16 games. One year later, Rogers pitched a game in which he retired all 27 batters he faced.

JUAN GONZALEZ — Outfielder

- BORN: 10/20/1969
- PLAYED FOR TEAM: 1989 TO 1999 & 2002 TO 2003

Juan Gonzalez was one of baseball's best power hitters. With Texas, he led the league in home runs twice and drove in more than 100 runs seven times. Gonzalez was the AL MVP in 1996 and 1998.

IVAN RODRIGUEZ   Catcher

- BORN: 11/27/1971   • PLAYED FOR TEAM: 1991 TO 2002

No catcher ever combined defense, hitting, and speed the way Ivan Rodriguez did. "Pudge" came to the Rangers at the age of 19 and earned his first Gold Glove a year later. He won 10 in all with Texas and was the league MVP in 1999.

MICHAEL YOUNG   Shortstop/ Second Baseman

- BORN: 10/19/1976   • FIRST YEAR WITH TEAM: 2000

When he joined the Rangers, Michael Young played in the shadow of sluggers Alex Rodriguez, Rafael Palmeiro, and Mark Teixeira. Young grabbed the spotlight by getting 200 hits year after year. In 2005, he led the AL with 221 hits and won the league batting title.

MARK TEIXEIRA   First Baseman

- BORN: 4/11/1980   • PLAYED FOR TEAM: 2003 TO 2007

Mark Teixeira was as dangerous hitting from the right side of the plate as he was from the left side. Each year from 2004 to 2006, he recorded more than 30 doubles, 30 home runs, and 100 runs batted in.

TOP LEFT: Kenny Rogers   **BOTTOM LEFT**: Juan Gonzalez
TOP RIGHT: Ivan Rodriguez   **BOTTOM RIGHT**: Michael Young

On the Sidelines

Few teams in the past 50 years can match the number of top-rated managers the Rangers (and Senators) have had in their dugout. During the 1960s, Gil Hodges and Ted Williams led the team. Hodges built the Senators' pitching and defense. Williams made big improvements in the team's hitting.

After the move to Texas, more top managers worked for the club, including Billy Martin, Don Zimmer, and Bobby Valentine. The Rangers' manager for most of the 1990s was Johnny Oates. He led Texas to the playoffs three times from 1996 to 1999.

In 2003, Buck Showalter was hired to rebuild the Rangers. Working on the sidelines and also in the dugout, Showalter was responsible for the success of teams such as the New York Yankees, Florida Marlins, and Arizona Diamondbacks. In 2007, the Rangers hired Ron Washington as their manager. He reminded fans of great Texas leaders of the past.

Johnny Oates watches the action with Alex Rodriguez. Oates led the Rangers to the top of the AL West in the 1990s.

One Great Day

The fans who bought tickets to Fan Appreciation Night at Arlington Stadium in 1991 wondered what kind of game 44-year-old Nolan Ryan would pitch for the Rangers. He had thrown 131 pitches in his last start, and the crowd could see his back and ankle were sore as he walked to the mound. Even Ryan wasn't sure what to expect. Before the game, he asked the pitching coach to watch him carefully—he was not certain he could make it through five innings.

When Ryan delivered his first pitch to Devon White of the Toronto Blue Jays, everything changed. His fastball exploded across home plate at almost 100 miles per hour. Ryan's aches and pains had disappeared. And he clearly had his "good stuff."

With his fastball hopping, Ryan decided to test his curve. In the second inning, he struck out all three batters with pitches that bent sharply over home plate. The next inning, Ruben Sierra hit a home run for the Rangers to give Ryan a 3–0 lead. That was all he needed.

As the fans in Texas watched Ryan, everyone began asking the same question: Would he throw a no-hitter? The veteran already

Nolan Ryan's teammates lift him on their shoulders after his no-hitter.

had six no-hitters in his career. No one else had more than four. Would he get number seven?

In the sixth inning, Ryan fooled Manny Lee with a pitch that Lee hit off the end of his bat. Texas catcher Mike Stanley slammed his mitt to the ground in anger—he was sure it would be a single. But center fielder Gary Pettis raced in and snagged the ball an inch off the ground.

In the seventh, eighth, and ninth innings, the Texas fans stood and chanted, "No-lan! No-lan! No-lan!" Mark Whiten hit a ball hard to right field, but it was directly at Sierra, who made an easy catch. In the ninth, Lee and White both grounded out to Julio Franco at second base. The final batter, Roberto Alomar, struck out swinging. Ryan's happy teammates rushed to the mound and carried him off the field on their shoulders. Ryan had thrown his record seventh no-hitter.

Legend Has It

Who was the first "perfect" left-handed pitcher in the American League?

LEGEND HAS IT that Kenny Rogers was. Like any player, Rogers sometimes made mistakes on the field. However, on July 28, 1994, he retired all 27 batters he faced against the California Angels. It was the first perfect game ever pitched by a left-hander in AL history.

ABOVE: Kenny Rogers waves to the fans after his perfect game.

Which Texas pitcher was injured by sunflower seeds?

LEGEND HAS IT that Greg Harris was. Harris was the team's best relief pitcher in 1986. The following year, he spent time on the disabled list because of a painful elbow injury. Harris admitted that he hurt his elbow during a boring game. He was flicking sunflower seeds at a friend sitting behind the **bullpen**.

Which Ranger had a rule named after him?

LEGEND HAS IT that Pete Incaviglia did. In 1986, the Montreal Expos took Incaviglia in the **draft** and then traded him to the Rangers. Texas immediately put "Inky" in the lineup. He was only the fourth player to go right from the draft to the **major leagues** without spending a day in the **minor leagues**. Incaviglia hit 30 home runs and became a favorite of Texas fans. Montreal fans were not as happy—they were angry that Incaviglia never played for their team. Major League Baseball soon passed a rule that said a team had to wait at least one year before trading a player it drafted. Today, that is known as the "Incaviglia Rule."

29

It Really Happened

Ten years before the Rangers played their first game in Texas, a pitcher for the Washington Senators did something that no one else in team history—or baseball history—had ever done. His name was Tom Cheney, and he threw a good fastball and an excellent curve. Cheney, however, did not always have control of his pitches. His teammates often wondered what would happen if he had total *command* from the start of a game to the end.

The Baltimore Orioles found out the answer to that question near the end of the 1962 season. On September 12th, Cheney struck out 13 Orioles in nine innings. That would be a good day's work for most pitchers, but the score was tied 1–1.

Washington's manager, Mickey Vernon, asked his pitcher if he wanted to leave the game. Cheney shook his head no. "Back in those days," he said years later, "you finished what you started."

Cheney stayed in the game and kept striking out Baltimore hitters. After 15 innings, he was still on the mound. In the top of the 16th inning, Bud Zipfel hit a home run to give the Senators a 2–1 lead. Cheney already had 20 strikeouts—more than anyone in history. In the bottom of the 16th, he struck out Dick Williams to end the game and give him 21. No one has ever done better.

RIGHT: Tom Cheney, the record-setting pitcher who struck out 21 batters.

Team Spirit

From the day they moved to Texas in 1972, the Rangers wanted to play the best baseball possible for their fans. Sometimes they reached that goal, and sometimes they did not. Their effort, however, never changed.

Starting in the 1970s, the Rangers traded away many of their young players to get stars who could help them win right away. Texas fans got to root for All-Stars such as Gaylord Perry, Bert Blyleven, Bobby Bonds, Richie Zisk, and Al Oliver. It was a fun time to cheer for the team. Unfortunately, the Rangers never finished higher than second place.

In the 1990s, the team put some great Latino players on the field. Millions of Spanish-speaking Texans became Rangers fans. In 2001, the club signed Alex Rodriguez. Many people considered him to be baseball's greatest star. The Rangers gave the young slugger the richest contract in history. "A-Rod" paid them back by hitting 57 home runs in 2002 and winning the AL MVP the following year.

Texas fans always appreciate a good effort from their players.

Timeline

Toby Harrah, an All-Star for Texas in 1972.

1965
Relief pitcher Ron Kline leads the AL with 29 **saves**.

1972
The team moves to Texas and becomes the Rangers.

1961
The team plays its first season as the Washington Senators.

1968
Frank Howard hits 10 homers in 20 **at-bats** in May.

1969
Dick Bosman leads the AL with a 2.19 **earned run average (ERA)**.

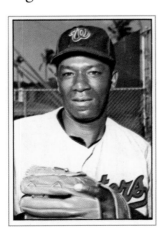

Bennie Daniels, Washington's top pitcher in 1961.

Dick Bosman

Jim Sundberg

Sammy Sosa

1981
Jim Sundberg wins his sixth Gold Glove in a row.

1991
Julio Franco leads the AL with a .341 batting average.

2007
Sammy Sosa hits the 600th home run of his career.

1989
Jeff Russell has a league-best 38 saves.

1996
The Rangers reach the playoffs for the first time.

2001
Alex Rodriguez hits 52 home runs in his first season as a Ranger.

Alex Rodriguez

Fun Facts

SWITCH HITTER

In 2003, Michael Young played second base and had 204 hits. In 2004, he switched to shortstop and had 214 hits. It was the first time in history that an infielder changed positions and got 200 hits each year.

LONG HAUL

In 1967, the Senators and Chicago White Sox played the longest night game in history. Washington won 6–5 in 22 innings. The game took six hours, 38 minutes.

DOUBLE TROUBLE

In 1996, Ivan Rodriguez set a record for catchers when he hit 44 doubles.

FAMILY STYLE

The last batter Nolan Ryan retired in his final no-hitter was Roberto Alomar. In Ryan's first two no-hitters, his second baseman was Sandy Alomar—Roberto's father!

FORTY–FIVERS

In 2001, Alex Rodriguez hit 52 home runs and Rafael Palmeiro hit 47. The only other teammates to hit more than 45 each were Babe Ruth and Lou Gehrig (1927 and 1931), and Roger Maris and Mickey Mantle (1960).

LOOK, DAD!

Jeff Burroughs, the first Ranger to be named AL MVP, coached his son, Sean, in Little League. Sean's team won the Little League World Series in 1989, and he later became a major leaguer himself.

LAST LAUGH

When the Rangers hired Billy Martin as their manager at the end of the 1973 season, everyone laughed after he predicted the team would be a contender and draw one million fans. In 1974, Texas finished second in the AL West and welcomed 1.2 million fans to Arlington Stadium.

LEFT: Ivan Rodriguez
ABOVE: A trading card showing Billy Martin and his coaches.

Talking Baseball

"The best thing any player can do is to let his teammates know he'll be there for them."

—Michael Young, on the secret to great team spirit

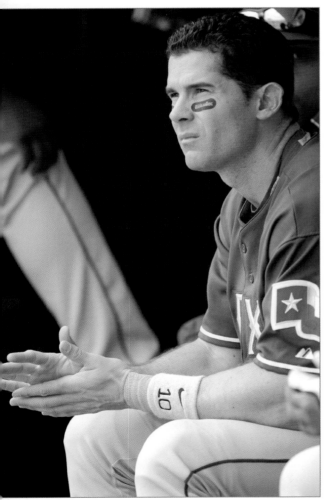

"Hitting is fifty percent above the shoulders."

—Ted Williams, on teaching his players the mental side of the game

"I hate losing games … That's not me. That's not the type of player I am. I love winning."

—Ivan Rodriguez, on playing to win

"To be able to play baseball for nine innings in front of a major-league crowd is a special **privilege**."

—Mark Teixeira, on the thrill of making it to the big leagues

"I think I got in the best shape of my life during the years that I was with the Rangers."

—Nolan Ryan, on how he was able to pitch two no-hitters in his 40s

"Move the mound in, raise it, dim the lights, and play all night games!"

—Charlie Hough, on what he would do if he were commissioner of baseball

"If my team could win and I hit .240, I wouldn't care. The only thing I want to do is win. That's what I play the game for."

—Alex Rodriguez, on being a team player

"There's nothing greater in the world than when somebody on the team does something good, and everybody gathers around to pat him on the back."

—Billy Martin, on the importance of pulling for your teammates

LEFT: Michael Young
ABOVE: Nolan Ryan

For the Record

The great Rangers teams and players have left their marks on the record books. These are the "best of the best" …

Fergie Jenkins

Jeff Burroughs

RANGERS AWARD WINNERS

WINNER	AWARD	YEAR
Mike Hargrove	Rookie of the Year*	1974
Fergie Jenkins	Comeback Player of the Year	1974
Jeff Burroughs	Most Valuable Player	1974
Julio Franco	All-Star Game MVP	1990
Jose Guzman	Comeback Player of the Year	1991
Kevin Elster	Comeback Player of the Year	1996
Juan Gonzalez	Most Valuable Player	1996
Johnny Oates	co-Manager of the Year	1996
Juan Gonzalez	Most Valuable Player	1998
Ivan Rodriguez	Most Valuable Player	1999
Ruben Sierra	Comeback Player of the Year	2001
Alex Rodriguez	Most Valuable Player	2003
Buck Showalter	Manager of the Year	2004
Alfonso Soriano	All-Star Game MVP	2004
Michael Young	All-Star Game MVP	2006

The annual award given to each league's best first-year player.

A souvenir pennant from the team's early days in Texas.

RANGERS ACHIEVEMENTS

ACHIEVEMENT	YEAR
AL West Champions	1994
AL West Champions	1996
AL West Champions	1998
AL West Champions	1999

RIGHT: Michael Young, MVP of the 2006 All-Star Game.

BELOW: Buck Showalter, the AL Manager of the Year in 2004.

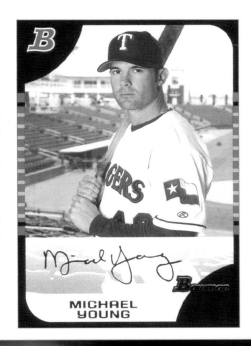

MICHAEL YOUNG

Pinpoints

The history of a baseball team is made up of many smaller stories. These stories take place all over the map—not just in the city a team calls "home." Match the pushpins on these maps to the Team Facts and you will begin to see the story of the Rangers unfold!

TEAM FACTS

1 Arlington, Texas—*The team has played here since 1972.*
2 Covina, California—*Michael Young was born here.*
3 Fort Rucker, Alabama—*Rusty Greer was born here.*
4 Savannah, Georgia—*Kenny Rogers was born here.*
5 Rocky Mount, North Carolina—*Chuck Hinton was born here.*
6 Washington, D.C.—*The team played here as the Senators from 1961 to 1971.*
7 Sissonville, West Virginia—*Toby Harrah was born here.*
8 Portsmouth, Ohio—*Al Oliver was born here.*
9 Galesburg, Illinois—*Jim Sundberg was born here.*
10 Honolulu, Hawaii—*Charlie Hough was born here.*
11 Manati, Puerto Rico—*Ivan Rodriguez was born here.*
12 Hato Mayor, Dominican Republic—*Julio Franco was born here.*

Al Oliver

Play Ball

Baseball is a game played between two teams over nine innings. Teams take one turn at bat and one turn in the field during each inning. A turn at bat ends when three outs are made. The batters on the hitting team try to reach base safely. The players on the fielding team try to prevent this from happening.

In baseball, the ball is controlled by the pitcher. The pitcher must throw the ball to the batter, who decides whether or not to swing at each pitch. If a batter swings and misses, it is a strike. If the batter lets a good pitch go by, it is also a strike. If the batter swings and the ball does not stay in fair territory (between the v-shaped lines that begin at home plate) it is called "foul," and is counted as a strike. If the pitcher throws three strikes, the batter is out. If the pitcher throws four bad pitches before that, the batter is awarded first base. This is called a base-on-balls, or "walk."

When the batter swings the bat and hits the ball, everyone springs into action. If a fielder catches a batted ball before it hits the ground, the batter is out. If a fielder scoops the ball off the ground and throws it to first base before the batter arrives, the batter is out. If the batter reaches first base safely, he is credited with a hit. A one-base hit is called a single, a two-base hit is called a double, a three-base hit is called a triple, and a four-base hit is called a home run.

Runners who reach base are only safe when they are touching one of the bases. If they are caught between the bases, the fielders can tag them with the ball and record an out.

A batter who is able to circle the bases and make it back to home plate before three outs are made is credited with a run scored. The team with the most runs after nine innings is the winner.

Anyone who has played baseball (or softball) knows that it can be a complicated game. Every player on the field has a job to do. Different players have different strengths and weaknesses. The pitchers, batters, and managers make hundreds of decisions every game. The more you play and watch baseball, the more "little things" you are likely to notice. The next time you are at a game, look for these plays:

PLAY LIST

DOUBLE PLAY—A play where the fielding team is able to make two outs on one batted ball. This usually happens when a runner is on first base, and the batter hits a ground ball to one of the infielders. The base runner is forced out at second base and the ball is then thrown to first base before the batter arrives.

HIT AND RUN—A play where the runner on first base sprints to second base while the pitcher is throwing the ball to the batter. When the second baseman or shortstop moves toward the base to wait for the catcher's throw, the batter tries to hit the ball to the place that the fielder has just left. If the batter swings and misses, the fielding team can tag the runner out.

INTENTIONAL WALK—A play when the pitcher throws four bad pitches on purpose, allowing the batter to walk to first base. This happens when the pitcher would much rather face the next batter—and is willing to risk putting a runner on base.

SACRIFICE BUNT—A play where the batter makes an out on purpose so that a teammate can move to the next base. On a bunt, the batter tries to "deaden" the pitch with the bat instead of swinging at it.

SHOESTRING CATCH—A play where an outfielder catches a short hit an inch or two above the ground, near the tops of his shoes. It is not easy to run as fast as you can and lower your glove without slowing down. It can be risky, too. If a fielder misses a shoestring catch, the ball might roll all the way to the fence.

Glossary

BASEBALL WORDS TO KNOW

AL WEST—A group of American League teams that plays in the western part of the country.

ALL-STAR—A player who is selected to play in baseball's annual All-Star Game.

AMERICAN LEAGUE (AL)—One of baseball's two major leagues; the AL began play in 1901 and the National League (NL) started in 1876.

AT-BATS—Turns hitting. "At-bats" are also a statistic that helps to measure how many times a player comes to the plate.

BULLPEN—The area where a team's relief pitchers warm up; this word also describes the group of relief pitchers in this area.

CHANGEUP—A slow pitch disguised to look like a fastball.

CLUTCH HITTING—Hitting well under pressure, or "in the clutch."

DRAFT—The annual meeting at which teams take turns choosing the best players in high school and college.

EARNED RUN AVERAGE (ERA)—A statistic that counts how many runs a pitcher gives up for every nine innings he pitches.

GOLD GLOVE—An award given each year to baseball's best fielders.

KNUCKLEBALL—A pitch thrown with no spin, which "wobbles" as it nears home plate. A knuckleball is held with the tips of the fingers, so the batter sees a pitcher's knuckles.

LEADOFF BATTER—The first hitter in a lineup, or the first hitter in an inning.

LINEUP—The list of players who are playing in a game.

MAJOR LEAGUES—The top level of professional baseball leagues. The AL and NL make up today's major leagues. Sometimes called the "big leagues."

MINOR LEAGUES—The many professional leagues that help develop players for the major leagues.

MOST VALUABLE PLAYER (MVP)—An award given each year to each league's top player; an MVP is also selected for the World Series and All-Star Game.

NO-HITTERS—Games in which a team is unable to get a hit.

PLAYOFFS—The games played after the regular season to determine which teams will advance to the World Series.

RELIEF PITCHER—A pitcher who is brought into a game to replace another pitcher. Relief pitchers can be seen warming up in the bullpen.

ROLE PLAYERS—Players who do a specific job on a team.

RUNS BATTED IN (RBI)—A statistic that counts the number of runners a batter drives home.

SAVES—A statistic that counts the number of times a relief pitcher finishes off a close victory for his team.

SLUGGERS—Powerful hitters.

STARTER—The pitcher who begins the game for his team.

VETERANS—Players who have great experience.

WORLD SERIES—The world championship series played between the winners of the National League and American League.

OTHER WORDS TO KNOW

CENTURY—A period of 100 years.

COMEBACKS—Instances of catching up from behind, or making up a large deficit.

COMMAND—Total control.

CONTENDERS—People who compete for a championship.

DECADE—A period of 10 years; also a specific period, such as the 1950s.

EVAPORATE—Disappear, or turn into vapor.

FLANNEL—A soft wool or cotton material.

LOGO—A symbol or design that represents a company or team.

PATIENT—Able to wait calmly.

PRIVILEGE—A special right only a few people have.

STRATEGY—A plan or method for succeeding.

SYNTHETIC—Made in a laboratory, not in nature.

TRADITION—A belief or custom that is handed down from generation to generation.

VICE VERSA—In reverse order.

Places to Go

ON THE ROAD

TEXAS RANGERS
1000 Ballpark Way
Arlington, Texas 76011
(817) 273-5100

**NATIONAL BASEBALL
HALL OF FAME AND MUSEUM**
25 Main Street
Cooperstown, New York 13326
(888) 425-5633
www.baseballhalloffame.org

ON THE WEB

THE TEXAS RANGERS   www.texasrangers.com
  • *Learn more about the Rangers*

MAJOR LEAGUE BASEBALL   www.mlb.com
  • *Learn more about all the major league teams*

MINOR LEAGUE BASEBALL   www.minorleaguebaseball.com
  • *Learn more about the minor leagues*

ON THE BOOKSHELF

To learn more about the sport of baseball, look for these books at your library or bookstore:

  • Kelly, James. *Baseball*. New York, New York: DK, 2005.

  • Jacobs, Greg. *The Everything Kids' Baseball Book*. Cincinnati, Ohio: Adams Media Corporation, 2006.

  • Stewart, Mark and Kennedy, Mike. *Long Ball: The Legend and Lore of the Home Run*. Minneapolis, Minnesota: Millbrook Press, 2006.

Index

The Team

MARK STEWART has written more than 25 books on baseball, and over 100 sports books for kids. He grew up in New York City during the 1960s rooting for the Yankees and Mets, and now takes his two daughters, Mariah and Rachel, to the same ballparks. Mark comes from a family of writers. His grandfather was Sunday Editor of the *New York Times* and his mother was Articles Editor of *Ladies' Home Journal* and *McCall's*. Mark has profiled hundreds of athletes over the last 20 years. He has also written several books about his native New York and New Jersey, his home today. Mark is a graduate of Duke University, with a degree in history. He lives with his daughters and wife, Sarah, overlooking Sandy Hook, NJ.

JAMES L. GATES, JR. has served as Library Director at the National Baseball Hall of Fame since 1995. He had previously served in academic libraries for almost fifteen years. He holds degrees from Belmont Abbey College, the University of Notre Dame, and Indiana University. During his career Jim has authored several academic articles and has served in an editorial capacity on multiple book, magazine, and museum publications, and he also serves as host for the Annual Cooperstown Symposium on Baseball and American Culture. He is an ardent Baltimore Orioles fan and enjoys watching baseball with his wife and two children.

DEC   2009

CLIFTON PARK-HALFMOON PUBLIC LIBRARY, NY

0 00 06 0349372 7